CW00421709

An account of a Cruise, with interaction from friends at home on a Whats app site. Dedicated to **Fraser Clark** who showed me how to use my iphone. With thanks to Bridge friends, Eleanor, Karen and Lesley. Also Alan Mackenzie and Daniel Rizzo for technical advice. Profits will go to Cancer Research UK.

TO CRUISE OR NOT TO CRUISE

30/08/2023

Hi this is Christine.
8.07p.m. Eleanor- Hi Christine, good to meet you. I enjoyed our Bridge partnership this afternoon. Looking forward to hearing all about your adventures on the high seas!
8.15p.m. Lesley- Hi Christine, have a fantastic cruise and I'm looking forward to seeing your posts and adventures.
8.30p.m. Me: I haven't worked out how to add Karen. Can one of you two do it?
8.32p.m. Lesley- I've added Karen to the group.
9.26p.m. Me: Thanks.

04/09/2023

9.42a.m. Me: The packing is done. I sneaked the Swiss army knife in for any little jobs and am now waiting for the taxi to take me to Portsmouth. I'm down for 10.00a.m. pick up, but had no confirmation. Trying to remind myself it's supposed to be stress free.

Feet up patio door open, waiting for pick up.

9.46a.m. Lesley- Don't stress it'll be fine. Have a great time and looking forward to your posts.

9.54a.m. Karen- Have a wonderful time! Hope your Swiss army knife isn't confiscated! My husband once packed one into his luggage on a flight. As you might imagine he was offered the choice to put it in the hold or have it confiscated!!!

3.44p.m. Eleanor- Have a wonderful time.

Portsmouth. See the ship in the background like block of flats on water.

Black silhouette of my head against the side of the ship.

Sampling the non-alcoholic Sauvignon Blanc, just the right temperature. Lovely. Shame I can't drink the real stuff!

5.09p.m. Me: The captain has just announced departure in low, slow, base tones of slightly slurred Greek accent. Suspect a slug of Ouzo has passed his lips.

The safety drill guiding us to Muster stations went smoothly. Mine, fortunately being in deck 11 bar.

Off for a meal soon.

5.13p.m. Karen- Chin chin! Looking very jolly and relaxed Christine. Who is your personal photographer for the cruise

5.45p.m. Me: Sadly, I don't have one.

5.47p.m. Lesley- What a beautiful evening to be sailing away on!

Eleanor- Is there a Bridge Club on board?

10.39p.m. Me: Yes, off to try it tomorrow.

05/09/23

8.26a.m. Me: Hangers swinging against the wardrobe door woke me up at 5.30. The horizon seems to be going above and below the balcony handrail as dawn has arrived. We begin the Bay of Biscay. Brilliant pianist playing after dinner last night. Bridge at 10.00. Let you know how it goes. Take care Lesley, Karen and Eleanor x.
12.31p.m. Lesley- Bay of Biscay is often a bit dodgy. Keep to the middle of the ship!

12.49p.m. On the lookout for wildlife.

06/09/23

8.09a.m. Me: 7 out of 10 games lost.
These people were born bidding.
Joining Beginners later.
Got my sheet music of Ladybird by Tad
Cameron to give to Jools. He gets on at

Malta. Bit choppy au jour d' hui. Misty too. Can my stomach hold porridge and wild berry compote I wonder.

8.21a.m. Karen- Yeah Beginners might be more of a confidence builder. Misty here too at present, but has been the same for the last couple of days, then hot, hot, hot!

8.39a.m. Lesley- Looking forward to your next update. Another glorious day here and a Bridge lesson this morning. I'll have to miss the club this afternoon.

8.43a.m. Karen- Ok Lesley.

10.02a.m. Me: Sounds like you are enjoying an Indian Summer and progressing with Bridge. I'm in the quiet library waiting for the next Bridge class, Beginners!

1.45p.m. Me- Ahoy there. It's still grey here, but blue on the horizon. We did Doubles this morning, Penalty, Take out and Negative. Don't ask me to differentiate. Not sure how much info was absorbed, derrrr......

1.56p.m. Karen- Expecting great things on your return, Christine.
9.08p.m. Me: A 71-year-old boogying with a 21-year-old musician on the dance floor. How desperate is that? Poor lad, is he paid extra for that?
9.14p.m. Lesley- Fantastic, have fun! Toy boy in the making……
9.16p.m. Me: Oh no. That's an awful thought.
9.25p.m. Eleanor- Photos please!
9.27p.m. Karen- Go girl!
9.45p.m. Me: You naughty lady.

Three days at sea before first port Malaga, in Spain. Time for Bridge, Dance lessons, lecture on Malaga, Table tennis, perusal of interactive screen in cabin and FOOD.

07/09/23

7.30a.m. Me: Just after the Musicians
left the concert area. Check out the
distant figures. Classic cruisers all. Last
night, had my photo taken in my black,
sparkly finery for the captain's first
formal dinner. Totally stuffed myself,
ending with a dish of lemon/white

chocolate syllabub. The only type of dream boat available, very indulgent.

7.45a.m. Lesley- Where's the photo in your finery?

8.09a.m. Me: I will try to find it. The photographer hangs out somewhere. This is a Big Boat!

He has a small office. Tall thin guy, folds up, to sleep in large office chair.

8.10a.m. Me: Deck shoes

8.12a.m. Lesley- We want photos of you, not your feet!

8.21 a.m. Me: Me and the Breakfast Waiter. Won't be wearing this top again! Where has the svelte me gone?

Tomorrow, the top will be consigned to small dirty laundry bag to fester for a few days in the bottom of the wardrobe.

10.37a.m. Me: Looking out for whales and dolphins and seals. Just saw a couple of Gannets. It is I who is becoming whale shaped. Cookies and shortbread with coffee and lots of goodies on offer.
Still passing Portugal today. Straits of Gibraltar coming up and first stop Malaga tomorrow. Brilliant industrial sized binoculars in every cabin. Also a safe which immediately says complicated technical object, to me. The

passport has to go in it, I know, so steal myself to **read instructions** and use it. Yay! Done it!

Couple of lazy herring gulls seen on departure.

Two more days at sea and have met a multitude of monotone guests. The grey/beige/cream/inoffensive pale blue people with pasty complexions blend with the outside where the sea is light grey/ mid grey, striated with ultramarine blue. Hopefully the sun will soon put colour in their cheeks, all of them. A very gentle sea, lightly lapping the side of the ship, swooshes rhythmically. Time for a nap.

8.27p.m. Me: About to go through the
Straits of Gibraltar.
Have joined ship's choir to sing
BeeGees and Abba songs. Microphone

annoyingly loud from enthusiastic YOUNG teachers.

Great steak in pepper sauce eaten al fresco see view above. Sun sinking into horizon.

Little tiny lights of North Africa in sight tonight.

08/09/2023

11 13a.m. Me: 28 degrees here in Malaga today. Done the quick bus tour. The border between ship and land means a custom's check on the lookout for Drugs. With us elderlies most of us had handbags and back packs full of them. Not sure Statins count. Fair amount of alarms triggered by metal joints. It's not plain sailing for old codgers is it?!

The bull ring at Malaga seen from the coach window on our morning excursion. What an incredible building. What a wonderful place Malaga is. Don't think too hard about what goes on in the B… ring. The guide on the bus finishes every sentence with a little hmph? Large piece of parcel tape would come in handy.

The afternoon was spent in Malaga. We wandered and found a bit of a dive. Therein was the magical fantasy of Flamenco. More later.

09.24p.m. Me: Came across a familiar face from a Great rail journey holiday I went on last year Not surprisingly similar types go on these holidays. Sat on a table with him and a very flirty ex nurse whose ex- serviceman husband is the most boring person I have ever met 'Oh we've been to Alaska, what you haven't? It's the best place to visit in the world'. Oh yeah and somewhat inhospitable and COLD. 'How about Istanbul? Surely you must have been there?' 'No I haven't actually.' 'They produce the most amazing array of vegetables there. You must go there and try it' No thank you the Moroccan restaurant in Bedford town does an amazing vegetable display plate. Thank heavens for the lovely Dentist's wife, who sat next to me. Lost her husband at 60 having been pulling teeth for 20 years.

9.28p.m. Lesley- Well I've been to Istanbul… hated it! I obviously missed something… or a lot!

10.47p.m. Eleanor- Someone like that on every trip. My tip is to say 'No I haven't really been anywhere' and then they lose interest in you and talk to someone else!

Me: Thanks guys feel a bit better now.

10.51p.m. Eleanor- Love the Flamenco. Fab! - to watch that is, not perform!

09/09/2023

6.30a.m. Me: Seeing the Flamenco was an outstanding moment. The passion of the female singer, chanting distant, ancient, cultural tunes, the guitarist with his fingers fluttering over the strings in Spanish style, the male dancer in his black costume, so elegant and proud, the female dancer with castanets clicking and stamping, whirling her shawl around, in spectacular and dramatic display. The boarded plinth was etched with chips and scratches from the foot loaded rhythm of sound. It was truly fantastic. Went back in a crocodile through the streets, then the coach back to the ship. Yesterday will be with me for quite a while.

6.33a.m. Lesley- I'm still boiling
Christine, in fact I think I've melted!
Cooling off at the moment with a
negroni. It's hot in good ol' Blighty.
I liked Malaga, walked around the old
town many years ago.
Love the flamenco! Thank you for your
updates with all the old codgers.

Ice cubes melting...

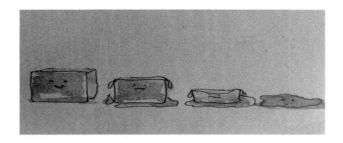

7.45a.m. Lesley- Yes, just like that
Eleanor. I'm melting too, I'm sure I left
puddles when I went to Rothesay
Education Centre today to enquire
about a course. Can't get on any I
want to do and their waitlist isn't a wait

list .... just a free for all... but that's another story!   Have fun Christine People can be really tedious with their stories of 'places we have been'!!!!

6:49a.m. - Me: See previous view from cabin of container ship not so dull with Brahms' German Requiem blasting out of my mini music system. That's me in a mood to break my routine of porridge this morning. It will be scrambled egg, fried mushrooms and muesli. Not all on the same plate of course.

I don't know what's happened to the Captain this morning. He just announced where we are in the Med and we are now racing along at a rate of knots, definitely not conducive to doing a bit of painting on the upper deck. My hat blew off, I dropped my water, the paint has smudged and my hair is all over my face obscuring view. At one point the paper blew off along the deck. I wish he would slow down. Hope you like my very poor efforts.

A light lunch beckons.

12.26p.m. Lesley- Where are you heading to now?

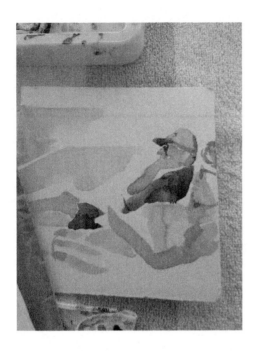

12:29p.m. - Lesley: Watercolours, looks like a man wearing a baseball cap and his hand on his cheek!

12:31p.m. – Me: Oh good at least you got the gist of him
12:31p.m. - Lesley: And photograph of the sea! Looks gorgeous. Still sweltering here, I'm off out to visit my

friend who's just had a hip replacement. Aircon will be at full blast.

12:34p.m. – Me: We are scooting along the waves to Valletta in Malta. Hope there's no Tsunami. I understand Morrocco has had an earthquake.

12:35p.m. - Lesley: Yes, Morocco has. You'll be OK as long as you haven't docked.   Sailing on the top of water is fine in a tsunami!

12:37p.m. – Me: You make me laugh. Am thinking about Hokusai's the Wave. Or was it Hiroshige? Know the one I mean?

12:39p.m. - Eleanor Very impressive!

12:39p.m. - Lesley: Hokusai

6:39p.m. - Eleanor: Ok I admit that at first glance I thought the blue was a parrot but I get it now! It's very good. Wish I could draw - my talents lie in other areas- at least I believe so but I haven't stumbled across them yet.

6:55p.m. - Lesley: Now I can see a lady lying next to the man, she has a white turban on with sunglasses over the top. He's got knobbly knees!

8:18p.m. – Me: I think I am beginning to gain weight. My dress was tight this evening when I changed for dinner. This reminded me of holidays as a child with parents we always changed for dinner. I was sat on a different table this evening. Not discussion about who's been where, more like all the moans and pessimism you can launch at the two other people on your table, in a half volume monologue. How ever I moved my head I could not hear the woman going on in a noise which I interpreted as being about her misfortune of losing her cabin key, how she wedged her foot in the cabin door, had to have it bandaged and why had the waiter given her red when she asked for rose. She had a disconcerting cast in one eye so you didn't know which eye to look at when she spoke to you. Along with a sort of droopy red nose and mumbling voice which moaned all the while. Glad I am back in my cabin listening to the swish of water rushing by. I still think he's going too fast past Algeria. No boat people or whales or dolphins. No spare men around to dance with. All the waiters are small 'Odd Jobs' who look like they should be hurling knives in a Bond movie.

Good discussion on how to use money... before 80 spend it!

8:23p.m. - Lesley: Still time to pick up a few Algerians when the captain slows down a bit, then there'll be a few spare men for dance partners. The young stewards really love older English ladies so you should get a few dancing partners to choose from!

8:23p.m. - Lesley: The ship needs to slow down a bit! Christine, you do make me chuckle!

Karen: You could write a book entitled 'Cruising with Christine and a bunch of old Codgers'!!!!

8:33p.m. - Lesley: I was thinking the same Karen.
10:03p.m. - Eleanor: You do have a way with words.

10/09/2023

7:04a.m. – Me: I'm looking into light blue infinity this morning. The sea is a soft, calm, deep blue. Still no whales or dolphins. Off to an inter denominational service.
9:51a.m. - Me: Thought I'd catch a bit of breakfast first. Always struggle to speak first thing.
Oscar Wilde said something very relevant about people who can talk endlessly in the morning. 'Only dull people are brilliant at breakfast' I think. Can't look it up as don't seem to have access to internet on board, at sea.
At breakfast there were exchanges of body deterioration over the coffee and

croissants. Denise was informative on knee replacements. The best knee surgeons are in Dublin for obvious reasons. Knee damage is a part of their history. Putting on a wet suit should be avoided with dodgy knees, especially when you reach 70 as there's every chance you'll struggle to get it on as XXL doesn't exist in wetsuits. Once wriggled into the zipper will not be under your chin, but scratching the back of your neck as you realize your pants are stretched dangerously up your crutch and you need to get it off and put it on the right way round.

The Playhouse service was well attended with poignant projected candle scenery. The ethereal leading role was well supported by the chaplain. I sang as loudly as I could and had a quiet cry.

10:09a.m. – Lesley: You do see life Christine or should we say sea life.

10:12a.m. - Lesley: By the way, I had a brilliant knee surgeon in Bedford and wouldn't hesitate to recommend him. Lovely man and he put together my 'smashed to smithereens' patella, broken tibia and broken fibula. I doubt many of those talking about their knee ops could say they were also put on a bending machine contraption for 6 hours ...... no doubt you are wondering what the hell that is!
Me: Sounds like a method of torture to persuade you that you do feel better when it is taken off!
10:13a.m. – Eleanor: What is a 'playhouse service? Pray tell?
10:15a.m. – Me: No church on board so Play house theatre where all the girls dance with feathers.
Lesley 10:15am - Oh, I see!

11.36a.m. - Roast pork comes to mind on observing sun worshippers on deck.

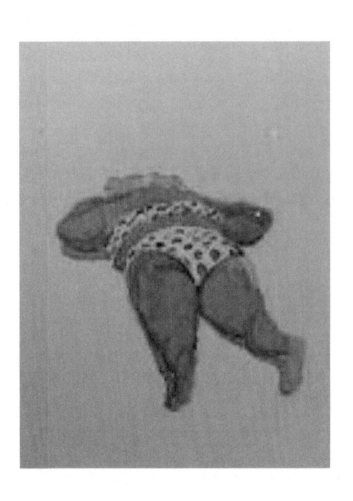

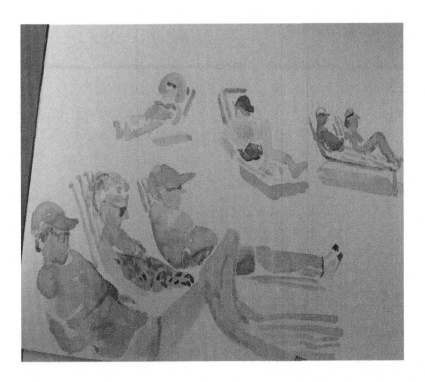

11:37a.m. – Me: This is what it's like on deck this morning

12:01p.m. - Eleanor: Are they all having their mid-morning naps?

12:03p.m. - Lesley: Are you with Jackie Gooding? I went to her art course last year, she's good but I couldn't get on any courses this year, even tried her course at Ampthill Rd ..... thinking Christine might like to teach me.

12:10p.m. Me: Yes, I'm okay with that so long as we could get three or four together. I have a summerhouse which lends itself to a bit of sploshing about. Mondays or Fridays are good for me. You bring the cake. I'll do the coffee?

12:11p.m. – Lesley: Yes, with Jackie. I was inspired by you and my friend with whom I went to Cephalonia. Now even more inspired seeing Christine's work. Cruising, bridge, singing and watercolours are all right up my street. I draw the line however at dancing with short waiters!!!

12:13p.m. - Eleanor: I'm OK with shorties ..... although prefer tall ones.

12:16p.m. – Me: I think shorties prefer tall beauties. Their eye level is more enjoyable.

12:18p.m. - Lesley: Great minds think alike!

12:26p.m. – Eleanor: You are so naughty Christine!!!

10/09/2023

4:49p.m. – Me: Lots of cruisers falling over here. Woman at this afternoon's tea dance twisted her ankle and had to have the contents of an ice bucket poured over it. G and Ts are now without.
An interruption on the p.a. system summoned stretcher bearers to Sunny Deck 13. I'm off to try out Foxtrot lessons in just a few mins. Mastered the Cha Cha with the help of a male stand in/ukulele teacher/semi-professional New Zealand football player. He seems to fulfil a number of roles on board. He's actually a 6'3" attractive 60 something. Hope he's helping me with Foxtrot. Valetta, Malta tomorrow.
4:52p.m. Eleanor: All sounds such fun.

5:00p.m. - Lesley: Ha ha, good luck with the foxtrot. All pretty boring here. The heatwave came to an abrupt end this afternoon when the skies turned black and the heavens opened. I went to Tesco to fill the car with fuel but arrived there to find it was closed ...... the rain had flooded the forecourt! You'd think the UK would cope with some rain .... had enough practice over the years! Anyway, glad it's cooled down a bit, I might actually get some sleep tonight! Looking forward to hearing about Valetta, has that been your first port of call?

Me: No, pay attention, we've already been through Malaga!

6:09p.m. - Eleanor: We just had a short shower and heard a few rumbles of thunder in Wootton, funny how a very few miles makes such a difference. My friends in Elstow mentioned hailstones but nothing like that here. But really enjoying the drop in temperature.

6:11p.m. - Eleanor: Hope you manage to stay on your feet dancing Christine! 8:10p.m. – Me: It will be 30 here as we arrive in Valetta, Malta. Glad you are all feeling more comfortable.

11/09/2023

7:39a.m. – Me: It's a bit frantic here this morning as Malta has appeared on the horizon and the majority are touring

on a timed bus. After the alarm went off, I went for an early breakfast and found a queue comprising another cruise casualty with wheeled Walker and large bandage on head. Sucked my porridge down and went back to the lift to down arthritis pills and prepare for ferry boat

to shore. Glanced the Great Train
holiday passenger across the gangway.

1:20p.m. - Views from bedroom, cabin,
window.
1:33p.m. -Me: We got on a coach to
tour. Mad rush by women with jumble

sale elbows to get the window seats. After 2 hours we stopped. We exited the coach to a beautiful smell of bacon sandwiches. Three elderly men watched us descend the steps and I tried out my only Maltese. 'Bonjourdy' I said. In chorus they called out 'Bonjourdy.' What a thrill, they understood...hello!

1:40p.m. - Eleanor: So pleased you are integrating with the locals.

1:45p.m. – Me: Once back on board I went through in my mind what else I'd learnt. Most of the year the temperature is about 32 degrees. In the winter it is like our summer. The Knights Templar are big in Malta. They grow pomegranates and sell the seeds as a super food...what for I wonder?

All the buildings have flat roofs and are very boxy concrete with some curved window arches and balconies. Whitish catacombs- ish. One stunning building with a twist in the middle by some woman architect with the name Zaha Hadid, I think.

1:48p.m. – Me: Now back on board, one guest saw Jules Holland and band get on the ship. I will now have a nap. I haven't done much, but feeling knackered.

4:13p.m. -Me: The meal portions have been disappointingly small here, today, orange pudding the size of a petit filou so today I was awake for tea. As I was told I would put on weight here I decided to work hard at it and stuffed myself with 2 scones, jam and clotted cream, 2 pastrami and pickle sandwiches,1 salmon vol au vent, an orange cream mini cupcake aaaaaaaaand a chocolate cream swiss roll washed down with 2 cups of tea. Now feeling a tiny bit sick.

4:24p.m. - Eleanor: In that order? You need to eat a nice green leaf, then you'll feel much better.

4:27p.m. -Me: Yes in that order I was overwhelmed by Philipino waiters all looking like Odd Job with plates of food on their shoulders, with circular discus, lethal weapon like trays.

4:37p.m. - Lesley: Blimey, that's scary, that scoffing is worse than me on my one day of the week when I'm confronted by the all biscuits that have been left out on Wednesday Bridge afternoon ..... munch munch!

4:38p.m. – Ha ha

6:08p.m. – Me: Just tried the dance class Tango - far too advanced for me. They slid and balanced across the floor looking very sleek and romantic. One couple looked particularly elegant and proficient, until she lifted her heel and I saw the price labels tripping across the floor in fluorescent yellow. How crass, no style at all. Maybe I'm just a little jealous.

12/09/2023

2:46p.m. – Me: Just been fox trotting with Derek the dance teacher and rushed back to the cabin because I am hoping my washing hasn't blown off the balcony. Interesting to see only women in the launderette today. Don't the solo men wash their clothes? Maybe that's why they're 'independent travellers'. Derek and Doreen are the dance duo instructing us. She has the neatly coiffed head of a ballroom dancer with sparkly shoes and tightly plucked eyebrows so there's only a line. He is very tall with red flashes on his shoes and an inclination to pull you in close so he can control your feet...that's what he says. I think I got the swing of it! Brian, the Great Train holiday man got pickled on red wine last night and revealed his side step side chassis while we waited for the lift. It could have been the sway of the ship, but I think he's been trying to hide the fact that he knows dancing. I know where to go for my next partner now. Jools Holland tickets have arrived for me, so I'm off there tonight.

2:54p.m. - Lesley: Ha ha, pleased to hear the dancing is beginning to pay off, in more ways than one! You'll love Jools, I saw him a couple of months ago, thought it was one of the best shows I've seen in a long time, everyone was up dancing.

I'm off to the pub quiz tonight, we won last time which was amazing as there's a group of six men that generally win every week so we were rather glad just 4 off us managed to knock them off the top rung! Fingers crossed for a repeat performance this evening!

4:32p.m. -Me: Good luck with the quiz, no internet roaming under the table now.

7:13p.m. -Me: I see a worker armed with rubber gloves and a bucket of disinfectant. He works his way across the carpet, rubbing with intent. We won't mention what fell on the carpet. The wind is whipping up outside and the boat is jiggling about. I have just enjoyed a pistachio petit fours with coffee and I wonder how long it will remain in my tum.

7:17p.m. - Lesley: Remember to stay in the middle of the boat, it doesn't jiggle around too much then.

10:33pm -Me: Put on my sparkly dress for Jools. He's a great entertainer and has a gift for 12 bar blues, but sadly Ruby Turner had a mic that she screamed in and I had to stuff little scraps of ball sized tissues into my ears. It was so loud. I sneaked out with another lady before the end and found a band playing on a dance floor on an upper deck with only 4 dancers. I threw caution to the wind which was still a bit lively and did a great bop. How long is it since I bopped? A coloured lad in sparkly, purple jacket and bow tie gave me a very respectable slow dance and another short, drunk chap tried to guide me round the floor. Not so good. I politely extricated myself from him and went on a late, night foray to find fruit tea. Strawberry and raspberry before bed. Bit choppy out there but I'll sleep. How did the quiz go?

10:41p.m. - Lesley: Shame about the mic as Ruby Turner is fantastic.

I have to give you 10/10 for giving everything a good go.   I'm currently practising Bridge on No Fear!   We came second in quiz. It was rather random with some of the general knowledge questions posing as some from TV and Film. The pub manager puts the questions together and she can never pronounce the words, bless her. Tonight, Mange Tout is Mainge towt!

10:48p.m. –
Me: Thank you for helping me along Bridge friends. It's odd being on your own when everyone else is paired up.
10:57p.m. - Lesley: Yes, it takes some getting used to. I've been on my own for 29 years! I'll strike up a conversation with anyone, but the first time I went on holiday on my own and started chatting to couples, as that's all there was, I might as well have had a big sign saying I was some sort of man eater or something, wives very suspicious! All I wanted was some company, other than my two daughters who were with us.

13/09/2023

7:44a.m. -Me: White horses on a deep
blue sea this morning as we go at a fair

rate of knots to Cyprus. Self-service breakfast a little hazardous as people carry plates full of fried eggs and beans skittishly catching their balance as they go. I think we are all gaining sea legs gradually.

7:45a.m. – Eleanor: I have great admiration for anyone who is prepared to travel solo! I travelled through Israel and across Europe as a teenager, completely carefree and confident but have now totally lost my nerve and so need to rely upon - and make compromises travelling with - family and friends. You are inspiring me Christine to regain my independence!

7:46a.m. – Me: Maybe we should all go round Britain on a Saga or Seaborne cruise?

7:47a.m. – Eleanor: I've always fancied one of the Fred Olsen Bridge Cruises!

7:48a.m. - Lesley: I'm up for that, whatever one of those is?   A cruise I'd really like to do is the Norwegian Fjord cruise, would need a balcony for that one.

7:49a.m. - Lesley: I'm off to art class soon, see you this afternoon Karen.

7:49a.m. - Let's look at what's happening next May. We don't want rough seas.

9:08a.m. - Eleanor: I know the feeling Lesley. Obviously any woman on her own is a man eater and to be avoided at all costs.

9:09a.m. - Eleanor: My sister did that this year, it looked amazing.

2:21p.m. -Me: Mainly a day of inactivity. We moved on another hour last night and my body is telling me to rest up. I went to Bridge this morning with John and Jane. She made an analogy between bidding in Bridge and being on her third husband. Didn't quite understand the relevance of making 7 tricks or 10 tricks in relation to husbands. One trick would be enough for me. John kept very quiet while she talked. I felt a bit queasy due to the choppy conditions and refrained from reading her copious notes. Blinking heck, homework again. Jane ordered him to get her a coffee while she went thru the notes with us. We studied them under her gaze and he returned with coffee with off milk. 'Take that back!' she ordered. 'It's off!' He went off to get one with fresh milk. 'While I am explaining the next bidding sheet get some fresh water too.' She said. With almost a gentle bow off he meekly went. He had learnt the first lesson of being with her in the Bridge class, the 'Yes dear' Convention.

He was allowed to take a few of us into the room next door for practise hands. He transformed into a tyrant, ranting at poor bidders and in one case shouting at an over 80ish lady. Jane's regression had resulted in him letting RIP on us. Absolutely decent bids meant we were

all very hesitant for fear of reprisal.
Thank heavens its Cyprus tomorrow.
2:25p.m. – Me: 'Janes suppression, not regression'. This predictive text is most annoying.
2:57p.m. - Eleanor: Aren't there any nice people on this boat?
3:28p.m. – Me: I have just done the passengers' choir and the lady next to me, Anna is in the category nice person. She has switched off email. Unfortunately, I did not and have just got one telling me to chop off the crown of the apple tree adjoining my neighbour's property. I do have a tree which is beautiful, but it is not an apple tree and I do not want to cut it down. She said I must reply that I will not be cutting down my apple tree as I don't have one, clever lady, problem solved. She had time for me. Don't know how much singing instruction was absorbed.

7:46p.m. – Me: Lifts are a big part of cruising on a ship. I started off thinking I would go the healthy route up and down stairs, but when you consider there are 13 decks you soon succumb to the lifts. It's an interesting place to meet other people. One sentence is all you can expect to communicate as the doors open for a limited time and unless you want to be trapped in for another trip up and down you have to immediately curtail conversation and get out!
10:17p.m. - Eleanor: So pleased you met someone nice!

14/09/2023

4:55am – Me: Limassol ,Cyprus.

Little pilot boat come to guide us into dock.

5:50a.m. – Me: I would enjoy being with the captain on his bridge. Following the little pilot boat

6:18a.m. – Me: A tray delivered to my cabin this morning including blueberries.

Playing table tennis, yesterday, as though I were still eighteen, as we all are in our heads with our 70ish bodies, was not a good idea. My back aches. Strawberry fruit tea was just heavenly. It's a while since someone gave me tea in bed and I balanced my bowl of cornflakes, blueberries and sliced bananas on my lap whilst watching the pilot boat guide us into Limassol. The calm reassuring voice of the captain with his Greek lilted language made me even more determined to meet him. He likes to give us twice daily updates on our Ship of Enlightenment.

6:44a.m. - Lesley: I always feel sorry for the older people who live in Limassol. Once, when visiting North Cyprus in around 2005, we had hired a car and went on a drive along the "pan handle" as it's called, had passed a few miles along from Famagusta and followed a sign to a restaurant down a dirt track road, came across a deserted beach ....

absolutely stunning bay with beautiful sand... no restaurant now! Another family were walking around, the lady hearing we were English came over and spoke to us. She told us that 40 years previously this had been her home but in a flash they had to take what they could carry and had to leave everything to move to Limassol in the south. It was the first time she had returned to her home. I felt so sorry for her and always feel sorry for all those people who had to uproot their lives during that awful time. The beautiful city of Famagusta lies derelict too these days. Political history has a lot to answer for even in these times.

No need to worry for you as you'll be visiting the South no doubt.   Looking forward to your next instalment of sea life!

10:12a.m. – Me: The land of Aphrodite says it all. No wonder the Brits who came here didn't want to leave.

10:20a.m. - Lesley: Lovely photo
Christine
10:24a.m. – Me: The bay where legend
has it that Aphrodite was born. She
married the ugliest God of all so she

was free to take the other suitors as lovers. She was dead good looking and had a brain too. The coach tour was the same rush from the ship to the bus. Once eased into our seats we all hoped that the comfort stop was suitably timed and that whatever precautions taken lasted. Miriam presented the talk with a slow Greek/English drawl. She sounded as though she had just woken up and one of the first things we were told was that wine and water were equally important in sustaining life on the island. This made me think that she was very hungover. As the coach continued a waft of urine seeped through the coach. I turned up the air conditioning and it just blowed it around!

10:38a.m. - More old codgers' accidents occurring. One woman lost balance into me on her rush to the coach losing her shoe and stumbling over. With an annoyed and painful ouch aimed at me???!!!

One poor chap slavishly managing his wife and her walker/pusher, not having a good time. Another lady on an electric seat got her flowing skirts caught round the wheel while going up the ships ramp. Go back everyone was the cry, she's rolling down on us. Two burly blokes in black and white uniform, with gold epaulettes dived to her, and our, rescue. Last two spotted invalids had arm sticks. There should be a law preventing invalids from leaving home. They are a liability. Worst of all we'll be the same as them one day.

10:39a.m. – Me: 32 degrees today,35 tomorrow.

10:40a.m. - Lesley: I'm laughing at the scene!

10:44a.m.– Me: Good certainly we could easily be very depressed by it. As me and others got in the lift there was a sense of urgency to get the door shut quick so the 'vehicled' lady and man could not get in and cause more hold up and damage. Back on my balcony contemplating Barundi for lunch today...we'll see. What on earth is it? Fish I think.

1:49p.m. - Eleanor: Hilarious Christine but you are certainly not selling your cruise!

2:41p.m. - Eleanor: I think I might give the Cruise a miss for a few more years!

2:44p.m. - Lesley: I'm going on a club 18-30 cruise.

2:45p.m. - Eleanor: One extreme to another!!!!! I think there are probably just as many injuries (due to alcohol rather than being an old dodger/codger)

3:53p.m. – Me: Now off the bus it was good to sit on the restaurant chair. I knew a short dress made me vulnerable to plastic, coach seat stick. My rear is recovering as I reflect upon the wonders of Limassol. Richard the Lionheart was the first Brit there. Known as the Coeur de lion he spoke French and married Berengoria, a local Neapolitan lass.

Shame to spoil the romanticism of the Knights Templar, but he turned out to bat for the other side (I am not homophobic) and she died early. I have signed up for an excursion in Palermo which is not so coach based and will chance it that the pickpockets will take one look at my shabby attire and totally ignore me.

Its Antalya tomorrow which I will try to paint...no coach tomorrow. Heraklion in Crete coming up, Rhodes, Sardinia and Lisbon.

A nice cup of tea now.

4:02p.m. – Me: I forgot to mention how I have been mixing with the stars. Like me, Jools Holland and the Hootin Annie band enjoy eating al fresco. We had lunch on the Al fresco deck yesterday. I heard that Jools and his entourage later left the ship, possibly to perform at a big gay pride festival nearby, in a few days. I think he and Ruby are performing.

4:05p.m. - Lesley: If you have the chance of a trip from Heraklion, there is the Palace of Knossos from the Minoan civilisation and the association of Theseus and the minotaur. I read the book Ariadne a few months ago about her brother minotaur and the Athenian who killed him. Also, they might put on a trip to Spinalonga, the last leper colony in Europe, made famous from Victoria Hislop's book called The Island, a fiction based on fact. The story brings a visit to Spinalonga alive.

4:08p.m. – Me: My goodness you are one well read and travelled lady. Thanks for the tips.

4:29p.m. - Lesley: Did you tell Jools that my neighbour has his motorbike?

4:32p.m. - Me: Blow it, I forgot.

4:59p.m. - Eleanor: I've been to Knossos - very hot and no shade so be prepared!

5:00p.m. - Eleanor: But Heraklion is a lovely city.

5:03p.m. - Lesley: Rhodes old town is lovely. I haven't been to Sardinia but it's on my list to do. I really liked Lisbon too, we took a private tour to Sintra, Cascais and the place that is the furthest western point in Europe. I'd like to go back there again one day. Quite a climb up to the castle area but you can take the lovely tram.

Food is out of this world, at first we indulged but after 3 days we could not cope (indigestion) and had to moderate ... a shame !

Restaurant: we could sit wherever we liked, we met like-minded people (often different nationalities) during the day.

On deck painting, at Antalya port,
Turkey.
See following relaxed sunbather with
open jaw and throaty gasp now and
then.

15/09/2023

12:14p.m. - Me: Antalya Turkey has arrived through my balcony window. I couldn't bring myself to get in the tour bus for three hours when the temperature is 33. Much better to sit on the top deck, listening to the distant call to prayer and having a paint. There's one wheel chair and a lady dumped on a cushioned seat. You need to enlarge the picture. The lady next to me is above.

I hoped I hadn't missed too much on the trip ashore. At lunch, haddock, poached egg, mash, spinach, carrots and broccoli followed by bakewell tart and custard means I was slumped in my dining chair for some time before I could move, which was good because the couple next to me said they had made the effort to get a shuttle bus to Antalya town and that once arrived they were dwarfed by masses of high-rise flats, 1 million 400 thousand occupants, and decided to come back. I didn't miss much on this occasion.

I enjoyed my time on top deck looking at the excellent mountainous view.

15/09/2023,

12:16p.m. - Christine: Foreground is the quoits deck. I had a go with a young-ish instructor, quoits that is and was useless flinging the rope circle right off the pitch.

12:17p.m. – Me: The old harbour is very attractive, with Roman Empire bits. If you stay there until the evening, the whole place will smell of barbequed lamb.

12:37p.m. - Lesley: I love your paintings, I've found doing those "running" watercolours so difficult, I love the effect.   Your ladies are really good too.

You look good in your titfer!

Think you made the right decision, scenery looks beautiful.

1:16p.m. - Eleanor: Very good!

2:16p.m. - Me: Thanks Lesley and Karen. It's good to know that normality exists out there somewhere away from the oven like conditions here where wind, speed of knots and meterage of swell are so important.

2:49p.m. - Me: The captain arrives on the tanoy with his deep duvet tones. To Rhodes we have 175 nautical miles to go at a speed of 14 knots.1 metre swell and 34 degrees falling to 27 degrees tomorrow. I hope I will meet him one day!

2:50p.m. - Me: It was supposed to be deep dulcet tones, but maybe predictive text is right this time deep duvet tones will do.

3:16p.m. - Lesley: I was going to say that I'd like to hear his duvet tones ..... in situ preferably!

3:50p.m. - Eleanor: Does he also have 'come to bed' eyes? Although it's far too hot for duvets these days.

3:56p.m. - Me: I haven't seen him yet. I will try to find out how I can see him. We have set sail again. It's odd walking down the gangways watching out for the walls to grab as every step is timed to avoid a sway.

4:24p.m. - Lesley: I've been on Azura and Ventura, both very large ships, thankfully I've only ever been on the long weekend cruises with group of friends, usually celebrating big '0' birthdays. Think I've been on Arcadia too.

4:40p.m. - Eleanor: That's taking the notion of 'come to bed with me eyes' a stage further!!!!!

7:43p.m. - Me: I had a pleasant meal in the Oriental restaurant and excused myself to get to the laundrette to pick up washing. I got to the lift wanting to go up. A couple, waiting to go up, called out advising me, as the door closed, that I was in the down one. Having arrived down, two people got in and we proceeded to go up. The lift stopped and opened where the original couple were and got in. I didn't recognise them until the man said, 'I think I have a sense of deja-vu.' I suddenly realized it was them and it was one of those moments when you dig a hole and just go in deeper. 'I haven't had a drink honestly' I said and 'I do need to go up one deck.' At this point the woman looked down her nose at me, the door opened and I escaped to the launderette.

16/09/23

A new day has dawned and I await the next event, breakfast.

5:43a.m. - Me: We are now in Rhodes. enlarge the background to see all the old and wonderful relics. Foreground not so wonderful relic. Breakfast delivered at 10 past six!

5:45a.m. - Lesley: Enjoy Rhodes, the old town is lovely.

10:35a.m. - Me: Rhodes is a well-kept secret. I don't remember seeing much in the way of advertisement for its wonderful sights, colours, kind people and climate. A large catamaran with waving people has just passed my balcony window. It's hard work being a tourist on a coach. Up at 6.15 for tea and cornflakes. Shower, dress. Pack day bag. Find excursion ticket, find proof of passenger card, find queue for customs, find queue for right bus out of 6, find free, water bottle 35 degrees today. Climb on bus, it is a climb, try to work out if best to be on left or right. Now back with swollen ankles and feet up.

Knights Templar still have a thread of existence, and went from from Cyprus to Rhodes and are now based in Malta. Gilmore of The Pink Floyd lived here for

4 years. He wrote Dark Side of the Moon here.

Anthony Quinn was given a beach here for his performance in The Greek. We stopped for a snack and an ouzo and we will stop for a relax, the guide said. Their hospitality was wasted on one guest near me who said in a loud voice 'Eeugh! Ouzo horrible stuff, takes the back off your throat.'

How insensitive!. I noticed the little black cat under the table skittishly veered away from him. After the snack I went to the facilities, whilst on my way back to tables I asked the guy to show me THE dance. Kick this way, kick that way then step behind and start again. Was just about to start again when I realized I was enjoying myself too much everyone else had disappeared. Panic nearly set in as I looked at the coach park with 6 identical coaches, all with blacked out windows. I took a chance and tapped on what I thought was the driver's window. He rolled the window down. 'You want-a bus-a one-a?' 'Yes' I said. 'Get-a on-a the-a other-a side-a', he said. Oh yeah, the door was on the wrong side, of course, I was on with only seconds to go before he pulled away.

After the twang of balalika music on board the guide took over and showed us two points where the legs of Colossus stood astride the harbour entrance. For 66 years boats sailed in to dock between his legs until an earthquake found his weakness, his knees. At 66 plus we all know that's a weakness. He collapsed. Only 2 columns remain at the entrance now.

10:43a.m. - Me: Rhodes is an historic wonder. How have I missed seeing these places in the past?

3:36p.m. - Me: Hi Bridge ladies, hope you're still there. I'm trying to organise a trip to see THE Bridge, but it seems popular at the moment.

3:58p.m. - Lesley: Hi Christine. Glad you enjoyed Rhodes, I loved it there.

We also hired a car and went to Lindos a few times.

Today I've been on a woodland walk on the Southill Estate, for anyone that doesn't know the Whitbread family own most of the land around Cardington, Old Warden, Southill etc. Charles Whitbread led the walk and told us that it would be 4 miles until we stop for lunch which was supplied, and then around a mile back. By my mental calculation that comes to 5 miles. Boiling hot day and we were marched up one of the handful of hills that surround Bedford by Charles, ex-army man. Fantastic view of the hangars across the fields and lovely trails through woods, I've never seen so many red kites flying around all at once (bird variety not flag types). Arrive at lunch hut, in the middle of nowhere, where coronation chicken, salad and jacket potato was served, with wine or whatever drink you fancied, followed by all sorts of home-made desserts, apparently there's always competition among the local ladies over who makes the best! The only downside is that there were no loos, only those behind a tree somewhere. Since I smashed my kneecap to smithereens I've been unable to squat ...... thankfully I have practised my pelvic floor exercises and have good bladder control!

Anyway, food was very yummy and we were invited to participate in the raffle to raise money for local church.

That done we marched back to cars where my phone told me I had walked 11.3km ....7 miles!!! I'm cream crackered now! Oh, and Charles plays Bridge!

4:04p.m. - Me: That all sounds jolly gung ho. Charles plays Bridge eh? What a great day.

4:07p.m. - Lesley: Will you be dressing up for dinner tonight Christine, do you get to see the captain?

7:50p.m. - Me: Dress up for dinner every night. Formal attire men in DJs and bow ties ladies, long and sparkly, that's dresses every now and then on a formal night.

19/09/2023

10:12a.m. - Lesley: Love it, dressing up that is.

10:14a.m.- Me: Here is Heraklion in Crete. The water is turquoise in the harbour and deep ultra marine beyond. There are constant aircraft flying over the top deck on ship. Big noise! I chickened out of getting a shuttle bus and going into the town for fear of not being capable of finding my way back before departure. When you are a solo traveller its difficult, Karen's right. Caution seems to kick in with age. If I forget the time again it may be tricky finding a taxi, but a miracle to find a helicopter to drop one back on board if you're really stuck and left behind. Ze Capitain, he waits for no one.

The port is cranes etc. The harbour has lots of little sailing vessels.

Feeling tired from all the luxury.

10:30a.m. - Me: There are binoculars in my room which is fantastic. If I peruse the skyline I can see little tiny jagged tops to all the peaks of hills and mountains. I guess these are the fortifications and Roman ruins I am missing on my day off excursions.
10:31a.m. - Me: The binos show that they are.

10:33a.m. - Me: My nephew sends me a pic of his cat that says home. Looking forward to seeing my little furry friends
10:34a.m. - me: Send pics of yours please do.

Sadly run over a few months ago.
Beautiful Sam
You'll have to zoom in on this.   Sam's
twin brother, Leo, beautiful nature, long

haired, sadly also run over 3 years ago. They were both half Persian and the sweetest, laid-back cats ever.

11:37a.m. - Me: Hopefully many happy memories of them

11:51a.m. - Lesley: Yes and I still miss them terribly.   No more for me though, The road out the back has become far too busy these days.

1:56p.m. - Me: The view beyond Heraklion port is low level flat roofed, pastel-coloured buildings, unlike Cyprus where the sky rise flats seemed to vie for space. Containers are parked on the vast concrete with shuttle buses waltzing to and fro across the huge space, occasionally blasted by the jet plane engines as they lift off and cast an ominous shadow beneath.

The sun is beautiful and I soak it up on the balcony.

2:01p.m. - Me: Sea day tomorrow and the next time for Bridge and the next dance lesson. I know someone who would hate that. Palermo in Sicily next where my lad loved to be, so much so that he left his motorbike parked at the airport ready for his return that wasn't to be.

2:21p.m. - Lesley: It's a shame you couldn't do one of the excursions from Heraklion, Crete is such a lovely island and the people so friendly. Didn't they do an excursion to Knossos or Spinalonga? I've been to Crete a few times and would love to go again. I'll be interested in Sicily as that's on my to do list too.

2:23p.m. - Lesley: So sorry your lad didn't get to ride his bike again ... hugs.

8:38pm - Me: Sea food restaurant, one of 5 was booked for tonight. The Philippino chef was challenged by potted shrimps, but his sea bass was 'melt in the mouth' with an olive salsa with capers, mash and asparagus. There was even a table of crew in their uniforms enjoying the fish. One had a pony tail scooped up in a bun. Just as they ordered and I polished off a lemon meringue, coffee with petit fours, the wind whipped up. I tried hard to keep my eye on the horizon, but whether the weather allows me to digest the meal we will see. I don't want to see it again. As the restaurant emptied I could feel the sway of a choppy sea. It was amusing to see people tottering this way then that way down the gang way, grabbing for handrails when necessary. There was slight hysteria in the air, like at a fairground, after a ride, before you throw up!

Back in delta zero three one cabin,D031, now listening to the spray on the ship side and now, having heard it, wanting a wee.

9:51p.m. - Eleanor: Hope the fish doesn't reappear Christine.

My walk - felt like I was in a Turner landscape
9:57p.m. - Me: I think you mean Constable, lovely. It's like Turner's Fighting Temerare here. Very choppy.
10:15p.m. - Eleanor: Hang on in there.

18/09/2023

5:42a.m. - Me: The sun has just risen over the horizon and the sky has a pinkish tinge. The sea is almost flat, I'd say half a metre swell, been here so long I'm using the sailors' terms.
My inside tells me I am missing home and missing all of you this morning. We are at sea for two solid days, goodness knows how Christopher Columbus did it. Did he play Bridge? That's what I will do today to occupy myself.
7:41a.m. - Me: Flurry of activity in the dining room this morning. Usual bowl of porridge with blueberry compote. The waiter, 'Odd Job' swans up with the menu and asks how I am. I say I'm missing my dogs. I ask his name, 'Frank' he says. For some reason he thinks he has reminded me of my dogs, no, I say, you're a bit like my son, who's looking after them, not the dogs!

7:43a.m. - Me: 'Are they called Frank,' he persists,' no,' I say, 'they are Toffee and Rolo.' Is he going to go away soon, and leave me in peace. Can't stand talking first thing.

7:49a.m. - Lesley: Perhaps Toffee and Rolo should meet my daughter's cat called Aero.

7:57a.m. - Me: The lady opposite starts talking about her schnauzer. I can't help but look at her large nose and wiry grey hair and see a large Schnauzer in her. It's TRUE what they say about the looks of owners and their dogs. Tho my ears aren't quite so prominent as my corgis.

7:59a.m. - Lesley: Aww, she's cute.
1:18p.m. - Me: 5 of us to play Bridge
was awkward as we chopped and
changed taking turns. It was mind
bending but I feel I learnt a few things.
At one point we had to find our score
sheet and, as we had about 6 other
sheets, we were all frantically scrabbling
around for them. Each accusing the

other of having them. This game encourages aggressive behaviour. In the end the lost sheet was found under my chair. I kept very quiet for the rest of the session.

This is the son of the other one. 8:12p.m. - Me: See next picture. The gorgeous guy on the left is The Captain. Captain Birdseye has always appealed to me. I asked Ze Captain if he knew Captain Birdseye. 'Who iz zis man?' He asked. I smiled and slid past, so he could engage with ze next guest.

8:13p.m. - : I didn't realize I looked so frumpy.
8:15p.m. - Lesley: He looks rather nice, a bit like policemen ... they all look so young! You look lovely.
8:15p.m. - Eleanor: Lovely photo! Not looking frumpy at all!
8:18p.m. - Eleanor: A floribunda between two dogwoods (roses) - because of their heights!
8:41p.m. - Me: Thank you lovely people.

19/09/2023

6:37a.m. - Me: Sicily appearing out of the mist this morning. Off to a place called Sestra today. Some sort of temple ruin 200 years BC!!! The gory side of me will be looking out for the sacrificial stone...

11:53a.m. - Me: Here I am at the temple. No sacrificial slab, but still one lady collapsed in the heat one man fell over scraped his knee. Does that count for a sacrifice? Diego the medic hunk assisted and she grabbed his muscular arm and strangely revived. Lovely little gecko things in the scrub.

Sang 'oh sol o mio' in the amphitheatre with one other opera fan.

The guide didn't look too impressed. He is a straggly long-haired hippy who boomed out facts in broken English which no one could understand. He made a dominant, horrendous noise which all 20 guests politely and quietly endured. It was fab standing on 5th century BC paving, but I would have liked to see the sacrificial stone.

Gecko see bottom right

11:57a.m. - Me: Blackened scenery from fires but also vineyards and olive groves.

12:00p.m. - Me: Hope that's enuf pictures for you. One more of Diego, The Medic.

Kind eyes

12:11p.m. - Me: Fancy being out at midday with the geckos in the scorching sun seeking out ancient treasures. Mad dogs and tourists go out in the midday sun...

1:58p.m. - Me: All back in coach to get back to port and ship by 2.00. The heat was getting to my brain The vision of a gecko munching on a discarded apple core made me realise how hungry and thirsty I felt. The coach driver insisted on taking us through the streets of Palermo in the vain hope of a tip. No chance. His monotone ramblings went on and on with every twist and turn in the road he lessened his chances of a fat tip. The streets were filthy and full of piles of litter. It was comparable to parts of Paris. I was too slow to catch a photo of a man in a check shirt scouring wheelie bins for anything useful. They seem desperate for money here. Someone suggested the Mafia might have caused this lack of pride in their town. A welcome sight of the hand gel dispenser met us at the ships entrance. We squashed in the lift and headed for deck 12, the buffet. I found a ham sandwich and the chef went to look for a tomato. None available he said. I also took a latte, non-alcoholic wine and water to my table. I spotted Angelo a tall guy, Phillipino. He looked me straight in the eyes and asked if I had everything I wanted, could he help me further? He hovered momentarily as tho he really meant it, so I said have YOU got a tomato? He disappeared and I paused my ham sandwich munching, anticipating a possible tomato find. He returned. No tomatoes. Somehow Angelo's tall dark presence convinced me he would find one. No such luck. Was there anything else a tall attractive guy like Angelo could offer me? I wondered…

2:01p.m. - Me: Tomatoes at next port he said, that's Cagliari in Sardinia, tomorrow. I am fixated on tomatoes.

4:15p.m. - Lesley: Those are two islands I'd love to visit.

I had my second Stained Glass lesson yesterday! It's getting better but I don't think I'm going to have any fingers left by the end of the course. I had to go to the first aid kit the times after splinters of glass left my fingers oozing blood everywhere .... not all at the same time though!

I'm off to see Life of Pi at MK theatre this evening.

4:27p.m. - Me: A boy and a tiger surviving on the sea, yes I can relate to that even more now. That's a brilliant film. Sorry to hear of your bloody endeavours. When its fired send a pic.

4:33p.m. - Lesley: I loved the film and the book. Yes, will send pics. I have watercolours tomorrow morning ..... shade and light!

4:41p.m. - Me: Looking for the light source is the first thing to do in any painting. Good luck.

7:00p.m. - Eleanor: First Intermediate Bridge class today. My head hurts now.

9:00p.m. - Me: I'll be doing the same on next Tuesday afternoon at Rothsay Ed Centre next week. I'll miss all the sea around me when I'm home. I may even have a bowlegged sailors swagger.

20/09/2023

8:07a.m. -Me: In Cagliari, Sardinia this morning. Still a comfortable 29 degrees tho overcast. Overeating last night, pea and ham soup. Angus filet steak with fried Tomato, yay, tomatoes at last, asparagus, creamed spinach, followed by cheesecake. Just had time for an orange from my room's fruit bowl and a croissant which I had squirreled away in the fridge. Grabbed my ticket for free tour and room card which acts as ID and joined the queue for the coach. Collected water bottle and finally found my way to a seat next to my Rail holiday pal Brian. It was sweltering in the bus. Air con off. I can't believe how compliant and reserved us Brits are. I looked around at heads all dripping with sweat. I decided to send a note to Diego our medic sitting at the back. 'Please get driver to put on Air con.' All hands raised above the parapet scrabbling for air con controls. Constant guide noise on poor amplification. Diego did not want to interrupt. All the while we were quietly suffering. As a medic he must have seen the dripping faces and finally requested Air con. The quiet was broken by a gentle approving cheer. Phew.

Ship in the distance

10.02a.m. Previous picture shows looking out for flamingos on salt beds. The guide says 'Here are the salt beds…… the flamingos seem to be feeding elsewhere or are just hiding!'

10:05a.m. - Me: Spanish influence church with tram lines about to be reinstated. I like Sardinia.

Stopped for a coffee.
The signora understood my pigeon Italian. Fantastic coffee. Fantastico!

Pretty obvious, cafe.

Tree.

11:07a.m. - Me: No more drama today,
back on ship. Time for a nap...
1:36p.m. - Me: By now you are probably
bored to tears with the holiday snaps.

When people show me theirs I'm okay for 3 pics, then my eyes glaze over and I fall into trying, yes trying to look interested, so if you are still following this, amazing.

I went to lunch and the waiter placed me with a guy on his own then he brought over another lady on her own. Feeling kind of worn from this morning I sat down for food and drink. The whole indefinable time became a haze of the small ex-navy guy talking about himself. Not for one second did it occur to him to ask the lady and myself about our experiences. No surprise he was on his own. I will avoid him in future. His constant prattle about the navy persuaded me to interject at the slightest chance and bring the other lady into the conversation.' And what part of the UK do you come from?' I said, as by this time we knew the life story of this man… and some. She couldn't speak. I think she must have had a stroke. She looked at me with doleful eyes and it was up to me to extract information by asking questions and her nodding or shaking her head. I'm used to doing this with my sister who has limited communication skills so I persisted. I wasn't able to shut the guy up. I tried looking behind me to avoid his eyes and stop his constant regaling of his life story. It was impossible. He would not shut up. My pitta bread mezze was miserable. My roast chicken had soggy skin and very poor gravy. Definitely a stock cube. The pink cauliflower was not at all trendy, just weird and the totally unimaginative puddings meant I searched for the cheese board all the time nodding and oh yessing and humming to the constant monologue of this guy. I put my hand bag on my lap to signal I was about to go, thinking it would prompt him to wind up and end. The other lady was not going to be left with him. She

too picked up her bag. We both pushed our chairs in and stood behind them. No, he still did not stop. I walked away. Self-preservation kicked in.
2:14p.m. - Lesley: I'm not bored with your posts, you're a born story teller!
3:02p.m. - Me: Thanks for the encouragement. A full 17 knots to Lisbon, Portugal now.

Southern tip of Sardinia, still no dolphin sightings

7:19p.m. - Me: Oh, I'm a day early. I'm all out with time, date and day. Must be a good holiday then I guess.

7:32p.m. - Me: Me in my 'finery' as promised at the beginning. Don't know why my eyes are so high in my head. I look like my dad!

7:35p.m. - Me: I think the photographer Photoshopped this. Where have my chins gone?

7:37p.m. - Eleanor: Lovely photo again Christine!

7:38p.m. - Lesley: Gorgeous photo of you.

7:45p.m. - Me: You flatters are in for a bit of stick when I get back!
7:45p.m. - Me: That's flatterers.
7:47p.m. - Lesley: When do you get back? It's been very peaceful at Bridge!

21/09/2023

8:06a.m. - Eleanor: Lovely pic - and a cheeky off the shoulder look
8:19a.m. -: You are looking very glam, Christine! Was it a special evening?
8:30a.m. - Me: Every moment is special here. That was a formal evening where all the ladies sparkled and all the men tried to, with their DJs and bow ties.
8:32a.m. - Me: Eleanor 'cheeky off shoulder look' you're a terror.
10:46a.m. - Me: 25 degrees here. Game of table tennis awaits. Bridge without teachers this morning. Man Overboard, I wondered, mind flashing back to instructions on the safety talk. In that instance one should prepare oneself for

a full decibellage 'Man Overboard!!!!' It should be shouted as loud as possible whilst pointing at the spot the body was seen. At this rate of knots it's not particularly likely to save anyone, I thought and where are the inflatable life-saving rings and the megaphone. Did I miss something…does everyone else know these things? I looked at the life belt in the bottom of my wardrobe and pondered the possibility of using it. I'm no good at puzzles, in a panic. How do the buckles work? I asked a steward what I should do. 'Oh don't worry' he said,' find a member of staff and they'll show you…and the other 900 people? I'm not sure that would happen. More likely we would all jump off our balconies hanging on to a steward when we had found one.

Bridge is un hosted this morning. John was very irate last lesson of Bridge, shouting at a player. His wife put him under pressure making him fetch and carry. We wonder if they've gone missing, did he jump or was he pushed off. One of the crew appeared and told us, ominously, that they had been put ashore. One of them showed signs of a cold...not the C word we were assured. I think they had had another row. He was her 3rd husband and they wanted a break from Bridge harassment from us, the passengers.

12:29p.m. - Me: Apart from sanitizing your hands before a meal it should be compulsory to visit the laundrette on this trip of over a week. The Phillipino staff meticulously squirt peach antibacterial gel in one's hands the minute we appear at the restaurant entrance. Having spent one and a half hours bidding and giggling with a group of 3 women and one man I think there should be sniffer dogs on hand to tug out anyone whose clothing exceeds acceptable B.O. levels.

The man next to me reeked. It put me off my bidding.

Are men worse at personal hygiene I wonder. My friend Claire always says so.

12:33p.m. - Me: Whatever became of John and Jane? Will we ever know? It turns out they were confined to quarters for almost a week. How they survived that I do not know.

2:02p.m. - Eleanor: So not set adrift in a small boat? John rowing obviously.

2:03p.m. - Eleanor: Maybe you need to carry air freshener as well as hand sanitiser

2:05p.m. - Eleanor: One of the advantages of social distancing and mask wearing was not having to experience other people's odours.

2:07p.m. - Lesley: Absolutely! Perhaps John could have taken a few large bricks in the boat ......"Oops, Oops Jane's gone overboard"

2:22p.m. - Me: Having napped have now mamboed across the dance floor with Reese a pimpled 15 year old looking Male partner stand in. He used to do a bit of football so was nippy on his feet avoiding my weighted wrong step very neatly. I felt sorry for him partnered with me as the girl staff looked on. Now sitting with non-alcoholic g and t. The magician has appeared from somewhere and has just put on his suspiciously heavy looking jacket.

My seat is just to his side. I hope I'm suitably positioned to avoid seeing where the rabbit comes from if you know what I mean.

3:14p.m. - Eleanor: Sounds absolutely enchanting

3:29p.m. - Me: He starts off talking about how he worked Covent Garden in the past and then for three quarters of an hour twiddled with elastic bands and cards. The PA was too loud and I have a slight headache. Most of the audience were men. I never have liked Magicians. He was like Paul Daniel's, very chatty, but precise in manipulating his audience. Going for a wander on top deck. The wind has blown up, swell is 2 meters and its distinctly choppy. Still no dolphins.

4:38p.m. - Me: Up on deck 13 its exciting. The wind is whistling through the railings and Perspex sheets are rattling. I lie on the sun lounger on my own for about half an hour, then get a mug of tea from deck 5. We are nearly level with the water. The three D quality of the waves is clear through the window and the horizon goes up to the top, then down to below the bottom of the frame. The quiet muzak in the background is irritating. It sounds like Winton Marsalis, which should never be Muzak. An elderly person has appeared, strutting her stuff to all of us sitting. Well- coiffed, shoulder length, blonde hair. It's so perfect could it be a wig? She's in a cream muslin floor length dress with gold embroidery. I'm a bit winds wept. Windswept too.

4:51p.m. - Me: A paper umbrella arises from the back of an armchair opposite. A lady behind that guides a straw into her mouth, trying to avoid poking her nose with the top of the umbrella. I sit up and get a better view of her tackling a ridiculously large cocktail. A few more dinner-dressed arrive. There are about one third again people here acting as stewards. Ask for anything and they will get it for you. Pity I'm after a pizza tonight. Venison encrusted is just tiresome. Now that does sound like a spoilt brat or perhaps I'm missing home.

4:52p.m. - Me: Venison en croute. It's that predictive text again.

4:54p.m. - Me: One of the Chasers is on board, big black guy.

4:58p.m. - Karen: The Dark Destroyer aka Shaun Wallace - barrister. I'm (sadly) a keen watcher of 'The Chase'!

4:59p.m. - Christine: Iryna, a Ukrainian pianist is about to play Vivaldi. I'll hang about a bit in my sloppy gear to listen. Alot of the musicians here are Ukrainian.

5:00p.m. - Eleanor: Love a bit of Vivaldi too!

5:00p.m. - Me: Yes Karen, the Dark Destroyer. He's presenting a talk this evening.

5:02p.m. - Lesley: Me too!

5:08p.m. - Me: Captain announces wave swell of 3 metres and wind speed high. Ladies and gentlemen remember to use the handrails. Cocktails amongst the guests with umbrellas and cherries on sticks and slices of orange cling onto the sides of the glasses. Let's hope they stay hanging on and also hope their tummies can cope. There seems to be a waft of bleach pervading the lounge already.

5:10pm - Me: Ze handrails. I have to emphasise his wonderful Greek lilt of an accent. He truly has a wonderfully deep and slightly rough (yum) voice.

5:13p.m. - Karen: I was a bit worried about maybe ZEERO handrails, a 3 m swell and a big bunch of old codgers O.D.-ing on cocktails, a potentially lethal combination. Now a little more chilled knowing they have zee handrails to steady themselves!

5:14p.m. - Me: Haha!

5:16p.m. - Lesley: I'm a bit concerned that the cocktail sticks might become embedded in the drinkers' eyes, or nose, when there's a sudden tilt of the ship!

5:21p.m. - Eleanor: Have you been on the cocktails Christine or are you listing????!
5:23p.m. - Karen: Or is it rolling, pitching or yawing?!
5:30p.m. - Me: Yawing??? Haven't heard that one before, but, yes, there is disruption to stability.
5:32p.m. - Lesley: Where's the next port of call?

7:32p.m. – Me: Lisbon Portugal.

7:36p.m. - Me: Not only is Jools Holland back on board, but the Dark Destroyer too. Lady at dinner said Jools was after pinching her freshly grilled toast at breakfast yesterday. As he leaned towards it she moved in with a 'That's mine' She had also seen dolphins. We are going through the Straits of Gibralta tomorrow.

7:38p.m. - Lesley: Is Jools still doing performances? Might get choppy around the Bay of Biscay so hold on to your hat!

7:40p.m. - Me: I don't know. We all seem to muck in together. He queues for food with his wife like everyone else. I wanted a pizza, but none available so they gave me bread, cheese and salad. It was good.

7:44p.m. - Lesley: It seems you have been cruising forever ..... are you enjoying it?

7:49p.m. - Me: I will let you know at the end. It's been such a long trip, over 3 weeks, I will have difficulty working out why I can't see water out of the windows when I get back. It's okay, but I am looking forward to getting home. Remember I am on my own, no family or friends to share it, just you lot, thank heavens for you lot.

7:53p.m. - Lesley: Just go and embrace everything Christine, which it sounds like you have been doing. Don't stay in your room too much. I always find the theatre purification on cruises have been brilliant. Have they a casino? I love the penny machines! I think I have an addictive personality so I have to be careful in those!

8:06p.m. - me: Tomorrows highlight activity on the news sheet, ' Swollen ankle secrets, walk in clinic'. I guess more of a plod in. Can't imagine what sort of secrets they would be.

8:07p.m. - Me: Former lead singer of The Drifters, Ray Lewis, in cabaret tomorrow night. Is that a Bedford boy?
8:10p.m. - Me: Not sure I want to watch Shaun Wallace. Its wild outside.
8:11p.m. - Lesley: On my message .... for purification read production! I thought that by buying new state of the art, all singing and dancing phone, that it would be a vast improvement on my last one with regards to predictive text .... obviously not the case! Not as singing and dancing as I had hoped!

22/09/23

9:56a.m. - Me: Its calm. A sea day
today, reaching Straits of Gibraltar at
noon. That means Bridge session, 2nd
lesson of Mambo dancing and lots more
beautiful food, prepared, cooked and
washed up with no effort at all.
9:56a.m. - Me: 25 degrees, lovely.

10:15a.m. - Lesley: Hope you're going to demonstrate your mambo dancing when you get back.

3:31p.m. - Me: This afternoon the Dark Destroyer got a disappointing score of 14 on the general knowledge quiz for geriatrics. Two 90ish year old ladies won with a score of 20! He walked past as he told me his score and I glanced away. During that time, by the Dance floor, one of the panels behind the lighting desk had opened and the disappointed D.D. disappeared. It was then time for Mambo lesson two. My partner, the ukulele teacher arrived. I think he must be on something. He's hyperactive. It's like he's circuit training. He's got his football trainers and shorts on. You remember he played for New Zealand. I had to take off my cardigan as it was getting hot keeping up with him and the teacher. For one moment I was horrified to think that at this late stage in the holiday my armpits may

sniff a bit. I tried to make out if it was me or him. Finally, I gave up as we sashayed left, then right. 'Open your legs!' he ordered and we exchanged neat little toe taps between my legs then his. Can't we have the music I muttered, slightly embarrassed by the sensuous overtones. At last the music came on and I got my twirl in the wrong place. 'Now!' he commanded. Get it in the right place, then, 'Cucaracha right, cucaracha left' he said. 'Heel, toe, flick and WIGGLE!, then, turn to finish... aaaaand............
start again!
3:33p.m. - Me: Phew.

Some of the holiday makers

3:36p.m. - Me: Some have cruises booked back-to-back. It's not unlike an old people's home on the sea. Comparable cost too!
3:58p.m. - Lesley: Hmm, think I'll give that one a miss! Gentleman in the shorts is pulling a funny face.
4:01p.m. - Me: We've been on holiday some time now. They are all out of clean clothes, hence shorts and ready for an afternoon nap.

4:39p.m. - Karen: I've heard that before - similar cost but food is infinitely better and no smell of urine!

9:01p.m. - Eleanor: They all look like they are having a fabulous time.

9:50p.m. - Me: Is that sarcasm in your humour?

23/09/23

Lisbon has appeared outside my window

10:19a.m. - Lesley: Ooh Pasteis de Nata ....yum

11:35a.m. - Eleanor: Skip the salt cod though

Lisbon,Portugal.

3:02p.m. - Me: Gave up the opportunity of an excursion in a crowded bus with 25 degrees outside, for 3 hours with traffic, roadworks polluting exhaust fumes and air conditioning belting out

for a. sit on the top deck doing a spot of painting. Ahhhh………
3:06p.m. - Lesley: That's brilliant, I could certainly do with a few tips!
3:12p.m. - Me: Noone available for independent travel, ie. walking into cafes and Lisbon shops this morning. Courage escapes me when I don't speak the Portuguese language and there are stories of pick pocketing gangs who circle their prey...the tourist and parasitically drain them of their security, I.D. ,Money, Passports etc.

3:43p.m. - Eleanor: Excellent!
Me- I hope you mean my picture and not the crime scene.

Elderly people on the pool deck
5:24p.m. - Me: Swell of 3 metres
expected tonight. Glad I got a 2 hour
nap this afternoon. Next stop
Portsmouth. Son tells me he can't get
central heating on. After a comfortable
25 degrees here today. It will freeze my
toes off if he hasn't got it working when I
get back. Still my lovely doggies will
keep me warm one either side of me.

6:03p.m. - Me: There is a drama

unfolding as we leave the harbour. A silhouette of another cruiser appears to be bearing down on us to the ships bow (front).Boom, Boom, Boom goes the hooter and to the starboard (right) appears a speed boat pulling in to deck 3 below the life boats. The little pilot speed boat zips back across the estuary towards land. The other ships silhouette has disappeared. It has gone from the bow around to port side (left). If there's no big bang it will have pulled itself well clear. Down below all the little jelly fish are gently bobbing around on our ships wake. Ahhh, still no dolphins.

6:04p.m. - Me: Is that our Greek gorgeous captain in the distance.

6:05p.m. - Lesley: Is that the modern crow's nest?

Little pilot boat sweeping off
6:06p.m. - Lesley: Captain has disappeared
6:09p.m. - Me: Captain's lair is a bit more appealing than crow's nest. He's gone to look out for the ship on the

other side. He's so cool, casual and caring with a touch of daring.

6:36p.m. - Me: Rang room service to get a few lettuce leaves. Don't think I am being careful with my diet. I am going for a big blow out breakfast tomorrow in time for the Bay of Biscay. Will my stomach cope? Is that tempting fate?

7:00p.m. – Do you think I am not enjoying myself? Being on my own is the part I do not enjoy, but its wonderful to be so spoilt here.

24/09/2023

9:40a.m. - Me: It's a 3 metre swell this morning and we all zig zag across the corridors grabbing the hand rails as we go. The lifts seem to work though. Everyone within is clutching at the hand rails with white knuckles showing. We don't want to be thrust into a close encounter without introduction. I get breakfast cereal with the thought that the milk will line my stomach and line up with the surprisingly large number who are after a full English with black pudding too.

The couple I sit with work their way through as much food as they can before opening conversation to interrupt my chewing, so my food gets cold and the mushrooms splutter out of my mouth, as I attempt to reply. We get on to wild life and I say I'm disappointed with the sad 2 gannets I saw. They tell me they met a guest who had to call reception as a bird had got trapped on their balcony. The steward took a hand towel to catch it and set it free. He did not anticipate the size of the bird. It was an eagle with a wing span of 8 feet! A little hand towel was not enough! He managed to disentangle it from the wicker balcony chair. A possible nesting place might have been the lure and it flew up to join its mate who was circling above waiting for it. Wonderful.

9:46a.m. - Me: Typing errors are occurring more than usual as I sit on my bed listening to the wild sea without, trying to keep upright. I am hoping I have my sea legs now and am not going to be ill. The Bridge players will be waiting. Nothing will affect our bidding and I have a strong resolve to keep it down whatever!

10:06a.m. - Lesley: Morning Christine, I assume the gannets were those sitting in front of you!

12:08p.m. - Me: The Bridge players knew more of the eagle incident. It was on the Chaplain 's balcony and it was a fledgling eagle, which had got tired in the blustery weather. It was just resting on the balcony, not particularly wanting to be rescued. It jumped on the balcony table and flew back up to its mother to continue its journey.

My bidding in Bridge was dreadful and we lost. Everyone hates me.

12:32p.m. - Me: Now in the Bay of Biscay ooeerrrr and whoops a daisy!

1:29p.m. - Lesley: What are those shapes in the sea?

1:32p.m. - Me: Will check later

1:32p.m. - Me Most likely nothing.

1:42p.m. - Eleanor: Surely only your partner hates you, the opposition would be pleased! Its true no one would want to partner you ever again, maybe that's what you mean.

2:12p.m. - Me: Ooooo you are a glass half full person.

3:59p.m. - Me: Crikey, looking back on those pics, I think those shapes could be wildlife! As I sit in the Lounge area, again I can see the horizon go to the top of the window, then to below the bottom of the window. The ballroom dance class today is the rumba. Yesterday's mambo was quite a challenge, but with the rock of the boat, a slow rumba sounds distinctly dodgy. 8 couples on the dance floor and me with Dick, Doreen's professional partner. My balance is affected and as she has told us to drag our toe across the floor. I am relieved my feet don't actually have to leave it altogether. It's a synchronised sight as we all topple in one direction, then topple in the other. Our faces are deadly serious as we all concentrate. I catch the eye of a chap in the audience who is chuckling. The waiters are dodging the wave swell as they dispense tumblers of water from their trays on their shoulders to the dancers. They are all Phillipino and seem to find balancing stuff on their head and shoulders quite easy. Bananas come to mind.

25/09/2023

10:24a.m. - Me: 200 nautical miles to Portsmouth now. The Bay of Biscay is now a comfortable 1 to 2 metre swell. Last night it was 4+ metres which resulted in a very familiar Captains party as we all sacheyed and tottered, for balance into the entrance to be greeted by him and his right-hand man Franco-see previous picture. I guess the staff on board must go through rigorous balance training as they always manage to skip out of the oldie's paths, as though they were lethal moving land mines. Lady's night at the party as we all boogied the night away. Live band with Ray Lewis of the Drifters was great. He had trouble being restricted to the platform so danced and sang with us on the dance floor. Hardly a high heel in sight as we all grappled with the five-metre swell to stay upright. Dancing with one hand on a supportive pillar in flats was necessary. One lady and I were determined to get a uniform on the dance floor. She queried the fact that they were all there. Shouldn't someone be on the Bridge? They had their whites on for the evening. It was 'An officer and a gentleman' moment all over again 'Haven't you heard of auto pilot?'

Franko said. The other lady was strikingly well-groomed wearing what looked like a Planet shot silk two piece. I wore my sparkly black number from Emaus and bumbled around in heavy, flat, black sandals. Sensible shoes is what I'd call them. We approached three officers. I fixed my eye on the one in front of me, Franko, and tried to persuade him to dance. She took the young cadet aside. They weren't keen and resisted.

10:35a.m. - Me: Until...I said, 'Just think we are your Grannies. Surely you wouldn't refuse your Gran a dance?' With that Franko raised his eyes to the ceiling, mulled over the thought, paused for a moment and visibly surged with the swell, to the floor. 'Yes okay' 'We're away,' I thought. Just a little tottering in one direction would be excuse enough to grab his arm. Hmmm don't let me get carried away. At this point Auto pilot time seemed to be up and they trooped off to the Bridge.

This morning I thought I would try just once more to join the 'See the Captains Bridge' party. Yay! After explaining that the ladies at the Bridge Club and friends were getting twice daily bulletins of this Cruise the officer doing the organizing said yes. So 4pm I will see The Bridge.

10:41a.m. - Lesley: Brilliant!

11:05a.m. - Eleanor: Yay! Pictures please!

11:06a.m. - Eleanor: I love an Emmaus top

9:38p.m. - Me: At last a space on the trip to see the Captain's Bridge. We went down gang ways we had previously been unable to access. The 10 of us were told to move regimented, on the right-hand side in single file fashion. We entered a door. It was a large room with lots of computer consoles and screens MFDs we were told (Multi-Functional Displays) and

lanky lads all around. A Computer
Games Club came to mind.
I still have no idea how the thing is
navigated. We were told not to take
photographs or touch any buttons. Do
you really think we would touch the
buttons?! We were guided and allowed
to see the most important piece of
equipment on the Bridge –
The Coffee Machine and there it was
resplendent.

Remember, no photos allowed on the
Bridge. Back to deck 11.

9:40p.m. - Me: The last day of the trip ends with the moon rising and bed.
9:47p.m. - Me: Thank you for being there. Lesley, Karen, Eleanor and friends.

26/09/23

Port of Portsmouth follows…

7:36a.m. - Eleanor: Welcome home.
8:30a.m. - Me: As I wait for my
chauffeur (in uniform) driven car home I
reflect on the last few observations.
Pulling into port I compare the beauty
and grandeur of Lisbon with the working
docks of Portsmouth. The view says
here is a totally congested and
overcrowded country…HOME.

I leave my cabin, Delta, zero, three, one and make a final check. Have I left anything? Have I lost anything? I find breakfast and indulge in the Danish pastries with latte. Theres a buzz in the buffet bar of the Breakfast restaurant. A lady walks by muttering, 'I've lost my husband! I don't want to leave my luggage behind, but I don't want to leave him behind either!' She disappears behind the drinks dispenser, on a mission.

We all gather in the Lounge to wait for our cars.

8:32a.m. - Me: Thanks for the greetings and all your comments. Looking forward to hearing about your travels everyone.

9:52a.m. – Eleanor: How right you are Christine. Our little island is absolutely heaving - so much more obvious after times away in less crowded environs. I think it's the combination of overcrowding and bad weather that makes us quite a miserable nation (at times!!!). Looking forward to having you back on our bridge tables x

Thanks to my dear son Ralph for looking after the precious dogs, Kevin, the gardener and his wife Jane too.

This was a cruise of a lifetime for me, on my own, on a ship, for 22 days. It was a Modern-Day Grand Tour for me. I totally understand why anyone would want to study Persian and Arabic. I understand why the son, who I lost, chose that path. The stories, romanticism, history and beauty of the Eastern Mediterranean are wonderful. This trip has given me the urge to visit these places individually for more time to immerse myself in the culture and incredible experiences they have to offer. The ship and staff too were excellent. I hope you have enjoyed reading my thoughts and those of a few friends who 'came' with me.

We still do not know if the marks in the photos were whales or dolphins.

Printed in Great Britain
by Amazon

33833710R00086